CRAZY STUFF
LONG ISLAND

LITTLE-KNOWN FACTS ABOUT THE LONGEST ISLAND IN AMERICA

Crazy Stuff
LONG ISLAND

Little-Known Facts About the Longest Island in America

CLIFF ROAD
BOOKS

**CLIFF ROAD
BOOKS**

Crazy Stuff Long Island

ISBN-13: 9781602613560

Book design by Miles G. Parsons
Illustrations by Tim Rocks
Text by Camille Smith Platt

Printed in China

TABLE OF CONTENTS

CRAZY HISTORY

After adopting New York as his home, Scottish sea captain-turned-pirate Captain Kidd sailed to the Red Sea to loot the ship *Quedah Merchant*. Upon his return to the United States, Kidd reportedly buried his treasure on Gardiners Island. Although some of the treasure was recovered, many believe that some is still buried on the island, but it has yet to be found.

◆

With Long Island being the second-biggest whaling center outside Massachusetts, whale oil was once so important to Long Islanders that they used the product to pay off taxes and debts.

◆

When whaling companies, such as the East Hampton Company and the South Hampton Company, boiled the animals' blubber down into oil on the shore, it smelled so foul that nearby communities passed laws limiting the amount of oil that could be produced in a single day.

At the end of a whaling expedition, the average seaman received the equivalent of $5. Though small by today's standards, that amount could feed the seafarer and his family for weeks.

◆

The Long Island Rail Road was the first railroad in the United States to put a steam whistle on a locomotive (1836), use all-steel passenger cars (1905), and install remote-controlled substations (1930).

◆

Sunk by an ocean liner and replaced by the British government in 1934, the Nantucket Lightship LV-112 is the biggest lightship ever built in the United States.

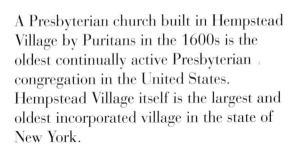

A Presbyterian church built in Hempstead Village by Puritans in the 1600s is the oldest continually active Presbyterian congregation in the United States. Hempstead Village itself is the largest and oldest incorporated village in the state of New York.

◆

During the 17th century, Algonquin settlers in what is now Suffolk County chiseled the currency of the natives, known as wampum, out of clam shells and later adopted the tender for themselves.

◆

Annie Oakley, Al Capone, and Will Rogers used to vacation in Amityville.

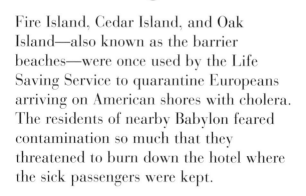

Fire Island, Cedar Island, and Oak Island—also known as the barrier beaches—were once used by the Life Saving Service to quarantine Europeans arriving on American shores with cholera. The residents of nearby Babylon feared contamination so much that they threatened to burn down the hotel where the sick passengers were kept.

◆

Farmingdale State College was once a home for pigs, cows, and chickens. It opened in 1912 as the New York State School of Agriculture on Long Island.

Full Ton Truck Assembly Company in East Farmingdale was so named because it manufactured vehicles designed to carry loads weighing no more than 2,000 pounds. Its name was later changed to Fulton in the early 1900s.

◆

Moviemaker Rudolph Valentino used Route 109, the old Farmingdale Road, as a mock desert for several of his films. Its sandy nature made it ideal for chase scenes.

◆

"Good grey poet" Walt Whitman taught schoolchildren in West Babylon but was known more for goofing off with students than for his genius. His antics were even brought up in court when a nearby farmer filed charges against his rowdy behavior.

◆

Amityville's Bethel African Methodist Episcopal congregation is the oldest institution operated by African Americans in Long Island.

◆

Built by West Point Foundry at the Bishop and Simpson shipyard in New York to weigh a whopping 490 gross tons, the *Steamboat Lexington* was never expected to end up at the bottom of Long Island Sound. In fact, the boat was only equipped with enough lifeboats to hold half of its passengers. But when 150 bales of cotton were loaded near the smokestack on January 13, 1840, its icy fate was sealed. Tickets sold for $1 for a ride to Stonington, and with 115 passengers the steamboat pushed off into the sound. When the fire ignited, it forced crew out of the engine room before the boat could be slowed down. Lifeboats could not be put into the water at such a high speed. Passengers jumped overboard using the non-burning bales of cotton as flotation devices. Second mate David Crowley crawled inside his bale of cotton, and it kept him warm while he floated for 48 hours before washing ashore. He was one of only four survivors.

Due to the lack of park-and-ride lots
and public transportation, 1,000 cars
were parked on the shoulders of Long
Island Expressway interchanges every
weekday morning in 1975.

◆

If it weren't for community opposition,
Long Island officials would have built a
four-lane upper level over the already-
crammed six-lane Long Island
Expressway. During rush hour, all four
upper lanes would travel the same
direction, helping commuters bypass
some of the rush hour madness.

After a mysterious explosion sank the USS *Turner* just 4 miles offshore of Rockaway Point, Long Island, in 1944, radioman David Merrill lamented that the greatest loss of the day was "a brand-new suit of tailor-made blues…. They cost me $49."

◆

In 1866, after making the trip from Liverpool, England, to Long Island Sound in only 7½ days, Captain Philip Cottier of the SS *Oregon* was elated. "Weather clear, seas calm, fresh breeze from the west, continuing at maximum speed. All is well," he wrote in his final log entry before docking. But his cheer was short-lived when just 22 miles from the Fire Island Inlet the ship was struck on its portside by another boat, later identified as the *Charles R. Morse*. While everyone on the *Oregon* was saved—it floated for 8 hours before finally going under—its cargo, worth a million pounds and including 300 mailbags, was lost forever.

◆

Nearly 283,000 people ride the Long Island Rail Road every weekday. It is the oldest railroad system in the United States still operating under its original name.

◆

Prince Felix of Luxembourg and his six children lived at the Long Island estate of Post cereal heiress Marjorie

Meriweather for 4 months during 1940.
The family was forced to leave their
home country after Nazis invaded
earlier that year.

Because of World War II, Long Island
residents were required to ration shoes
starting in 1943. Only those who could
produce a special coupon, number 17,
could purchase shoes, but even then
they had to wait at least 4 months to
receive a single pair.

The song "God Bless America" was
written by Irving Berlin while he was
stationed on Long Island during World

CRAZY PLACES

Flanders, Long Island, duck farmer Martin Maurer was on vacation in California when he stopped at a roadside snack bar shaped like a giant coffeepot. Inspired by the interesting means of advertising, he returned home, tied a cooked chicken carcass and a live duck to a perch for reference, and told carpenter George Reeve to get to work.

Complete with concrete feathers and eyes made out of taillights from a Model T Ford, Maurer used the building to sell duck eggs produced on his farm. Today the finished farm building stands 20 feet tall and 30 feet wide. Maurer changed the name of his farm to Big Duck Ranch, and in 1931, *Popular Mechanics* magazine named it The Most Spectacular Piece of Cement Work of that year.

◆

A Long Island radio station used to broadcast the voice of Christie Brinkley giving a first-person detailed history of Martin Maurer's big cement duck building in Flanders. The duck is commonly referred to as a "she," although the way the animal is holding its tail implies that it is in fact male.

◆

Every Christmas, the Big Duck building in Flanders is covered with lights and lit up like a Christmas tree.

◆

Octopuses, such as the giant Pacific octopus at Atlantis Marine World Aquarium, can be trained to perform specific tasks by watching the behavior of other octopuses. The aquarium's electric eel, which can generate up to 600 volts of electricity, is more closely related to the goldfish than an actual eel.

As a child, President Theodore Roosevelt came to Oyster Bay, Long Island, on summer vacations with his family to hike, row, swim, and ride horses. In his 20s, he decided to move there permanently, building a home on some farmland in Cove Neck just east of the village. He nearly abandoned the project when his wife, Alice, died just 2 days after giving birth to their daughter, but friends and family convinced him to live there regardless.

◆

The 109,000-square-foot Oheka Castle in Huntington has 126 rooms and was once the second-largest private home in the United States. Railroad mogul Otto Herman Kahn built the complex after being denied membership at a local country club.

◆

Arsonists have tried to destroy Oheka Castle in Huntington on several occasions, but it was built with fireproof concrete. Even the library shelves, which look like wood, were made of concrete.

◆

The Knollwood estate in Muttontown was originally built for Wall Street mogul Charles Hudson, but after rumors spread that Albania's King Zog had fled his country and lived there, hiding his national treasure in the walls, vandals caused such damage that the entire 60-room castle had to be torn down. No treasure was found.

◆

The Lutz family, who moved into the infamous Amityville Horror House at 112 Ocean Avenue a year after 24-year-old Ronald DeFeo murdered his family in 1974, moved back out after just 28 days, citing a serious haunting. According to their priest, as he blessed the house, a strange voice shouted at him to get out, and as he drove back to the church, both the right door and hood of his car flew open. When a friend came to help, his windshield wipers came on spontaneously and refused to quit. During the month they lived there, Mrs. Lutz claimed to have levitated above her bed, seen green slime ooze from the ceiling, seen the crucifix in her closet rotate upside down, witnessed her toilet water turn black, and watched locked windows and doors fly open and shut on their own. The family who lives there today has changed the number on the mailbox and claim it has been peaceful so far.

◆

The abandoned Telefunken complex in Sayville was used by Germans in World War I to disrupt radio signals, leading to the sinking of the *Lusitania* in 1915. Built in 1911, it was one of the most advanced wireless stations in the world. While it's in shambles today, it is still home to excavation sites, a labyrinth of trails, piles of old electronics, and even milk jugs from companies no longer in existence.

◆

Young fictional sleuths Joe and Frank Hardy of *The Hardy Boys* are from Bayport, Long Island.

◆

The Audrey Hepburn and Humphrey Bogart movie *Sabrina* was partially filmed in Glen Cove and Nassau County.

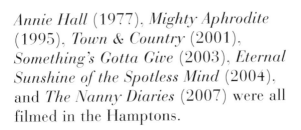

Annie Hall (1977), *Mighty Aphrodite* (1995), *Town & Country* (2001), *Something's Gotta Give* (2003), *Eternal Sunshine of the Spotless Mind* (2004), and *The Nanny Diaries* (2007) were all filmed in the Hamptons.

◆

Jones Beach State Park was originally just 2 feet above sea level. Following months of work, the stinky swampland was raised to 12 feet above sea level after developers dug out extra sand from beneath the ocean.

The first female swimsuit cover of *Sports Illustrated* (August 30, 1954) was photographed on Jones Beach. The issue sold for 25 cents.

◆

Famous brothers Alec, Daniel, and William Baldwin all worked as lifeguards on Jones Beach.

◆

On July 3, 1921, naturalist John Treadwell Nichols noted in his journal the discovery of a 21-year-old male Eastern box turtle at William Floyd Estate, where Nichols spent summers with his wife and children. He carved the code "JN21 21" into its belly and

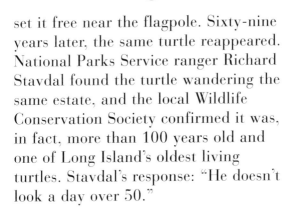

set it free near the flagpole. Sixty-nine years later, the same turtle reappeared. National Parks Service ranger Richard Stavdal found the turtle wandering the same estate, and the local Wildlife Conservation Society confirmed it was, in fact, more than 100 years old and one of Long Island's oldest living turtles. Stavdal's response: "He doesn't look a day over 50."

♦

American art collector Peggy Guggenheim gave married artists Jackson Pollock and Lee Krasner the $2,000 down payment on their Long Island home in exchange for paintings.

In 1918, a 90-pound chimpanzee escaped from a ship docked at Port Jefferson Harbor. The chimpanzee strolled through Smithtown frightening residents, and it was even accused of killing people. Eventually the town of Smithtown paid William C. Clark $16.90 to find and kill the chimpanzee.

◆

The Nassau County Aquatic Center at Eisenhower Park houses the largest swimming pool in the northern hemisphere; the pool stretches 68 meters in length. While many national and international swimming records have been set at the Aquatic Center, the world record for underwater hula hooping was set here as well. In August

2007, Ashrita Furman hula hooped underwater in the Aquatic Center's pool for 2 minutes and 38 seconds.

CRAZY FAMOUS PEOPLE

East Meadow's famous magician Criss Angel holds the world record for the quickest straitjacket escape (2 minutes, 30 seconds) and longest time submerged under water (24 hours). He has a cat named Hammie and a seventh-degree black belt. One of his mottos is, "Pain is a beautiful thing. When you feel pain, you know you're alive."

◆

Best known for his role in the *Kojak* television series from 1973 to 1978, actor Telly Savalas, a Garden City native, was supposed to star in the movie *Cool Hand Luke*, but the boat he was taking from Europe was slow and he refused to fly, so directors gave the role to Paul Newman at the last minute.

◆

Garden City's Telly Savalas constantly sucked on lollipops while filming *Kojak* because he was trying to quit smoking.

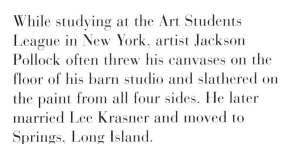

While studying at the Art Students League in New York, artist Jackson Pollock often threw his canvases on the floor of his barn studio and slathered on the paint from all four sides. He later married Lee Krasner and moved to Springs, Long Island.

◆

After growing up roaming the streets of Hicksville with a leather jacket-toting street gang, musician Billy Joel received criticism for his first solo album, *Cold Spring Harbor*, because his tapes were accidentally sped up in production, making his voice sound high-pitched and nasal.

New York socialite, Hampton resident, and
cousin of Jacqueline Kennedy Onassis,
Edith Ewing Bouvier once admitted that
she wished she had sung the soprano solo
at her lavish 1917 wedding instead of
asking someone else to sing it.

◆

Edith Bouvier's husband, Phelan, issued
her a divorce via telegram from Mexico in
1946. Their daughter, Little Edie, said
that because his method was not
approved by the Catholic church, it was a
"fake Mexican divorce."

◆

Edith Bouvier Beale and her daughter
"Little" Edie generated media attention

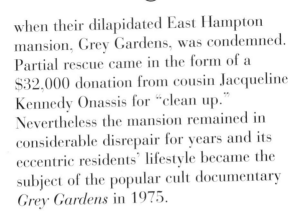

when their dilapidated East Hampton mansion, Grey Gardens, was condemned. Partial rescue came in the form of a $32,000 donation from cousin Jacqueline Kennedy Onassis for "clean up." Nevertheless the mansion remained in considerable disrepair for years and its eccentric residents' lifestyle became the subject of the popular cult documentary *Grey Gardens* in 1975.

◆

Long Island native Alec Baldwin worked as a busboy at Studio 54 and is one of only two actors with standing invitations to host *Saturday Night Live*. The other celebrity for whom the door is always open is fellow New Yorker Christopher Walken.

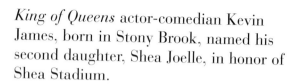

King of Queens actor-comedian Kevin James, born in Stony Brook, named his second daughter, Shea Joelle, in honor of Shea Stadium.

◆

Shock-jock deejay Howard Stern, who grew up in Roosevelt, ran for governor of New York in 1994 but dropped out when he realized he had to comply with financial disclosure requirements.

◆

Glen Cove-born R&B artist Ashanti was named after an empire in Ghana, where women are influential and respected.

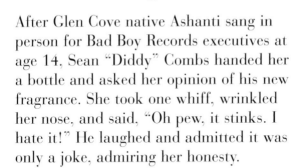

After Glen Cove native Ashanti sang in person for Bad Boy Records executives at age 14, Sean "Diddy" Combs handed her a bottle and asked her opinion of his new fragrance. She took one whiff, wrinkled her nose, and said, "Oh pew, it stinks. I hate it!" He laughed and admitted it was only a joke, admiring her honesty.

◆

Uniondale rapper Busta Rhymes started growing his signature dreadlocks in December 1989 and did not cut them until November 2005, in a barbershop later featured on MTV's *The Shop*. "I signed my deal and said I ain't combing my hair no more. I don't have to," he said.

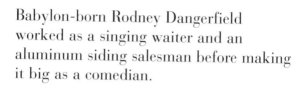

Babylon-born Rodney Dangerfield worked as a singing waiter and an aluminum siding salesman before making it big as a comedian.

◆

Amityville-born infielder Tony Graffanino changed the spelling of his last name—which used to be Graffagnino—after minor league announcers just couldn't get the pronunciation right.

◆

The Foreign Man character of Long Islander Andy Kaufman impressed the producers of ABC's *Taxi* so much that they wrote him into the sitcom as Latka Gravas. But Kaufman was so erratic in his acting that they had to give Latka a multiple personality disorder to explain the actor's sudden changes into other random characters. When audiences heckled him for not giving them the Foreign Man they knew and loved, he would fight back, announcing that he would punish their disrespect by reading them F. Scott Fitzgerald's *The Great Gatsby*. After a few pages, Kaufman would take a vote—would they like for him to continue reading or put on a record? When the audience chose the record, he would turn on a recording of himself continuing *The Great Gatsby* where he had just left off.

Producer Judd Apatow from Syosset wrote the initial script for *Knocked Up* during his free time on the set of *Talladega Nights*.

◆

Ben and Jerry's mogul Jerry Greenfield grew up on Long Island and met former business partner Ben Cohen in gym class at Merrick Avenue Middle School in Merrick, New York, when both boys were being chastised by their teacher for running the mile too slowly.

◆

To keep from losing his house in his bankruptcy case, New York Lehman Brothers chief executive Richard Fuld sold his $13.3 million Florida mansion to his wife for just $100 in November 2008. He had taken in $484 million in pay over the last 8 years.

♦

Legend holds that author F. Scott Fitzgerald modeled *The Great Gatsby's* fictional town of West Egg (where protagonist Nick lived) after his hometown of Great Neck and characters Daisy and Tom's town of East Egg after Sands Point.

♦

Tired of Long Island tax dollars being used across the entire state of New York, Suffolk County Comptroller Joseph Sawicki announced a plan on March 28,

2008, to make Long Island the 51st state of the United States of America.

◆

Pastor Bertrand Crabbe of True North Community Church in Port Jefferson used to joke with his congregation about how they would not be investing in new facilities "unless God drops a couple million on us." In August 2008 he got his wish. A church member won $3 million in the Bada-Bling scratch-off lottery and forwarded the entire check to the parish. The price the loyal parishioner paid to play? Just $10.

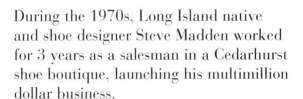

During the 1970s, Long Island native and shoe designer Steve Madden worked for 3 years as a salesman in a Cedarhurst shoe boutique, launching his multimillion dollar business.

◆

A native of Long Island, Michael Kors opened his first clothing boutique in his Merrick, Long Island, basement. The items available for purchase included T-shirts and leather vests.

◆

Twelve-year-old Leanna Archer, who lives on Long Island, started her own hair product line, Leanna's Inc., in 2004, when she was only 8 years old. Leanna and her family make the products by hand on weekends and fill orders during the week.

◆

In 1999, Southold resident Edward Munson filed for a patent for a new and improved mailing system. Recognizing that each location on the globe has a unique longitude and latitude, Munson felt that adding the longitudes and latitudes to existing ZIP codes would increase the efficiency of the current mailing system. Since being granted his patent, Munson has worked with several organizations in an attempt to implement his detailed system.

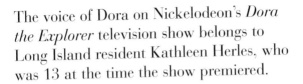

The voice of Dora on Nickelodeon's *Dora the Explorer* television show belongs to Long Island resident Kathleen Herles, who was 13 at the time the show premiered.

◆

Born in Huntington, Mariah Carey once worked as a hair sweeper in a hair salon and a coat checker at a Manhattan restaurant. Her high school nickname was Mirage because she never went to class.

◆

Bay Shore native LL Cool J was born James Todd Smith. At age 4, he watched his father shoot his mother and grandfather. He worked as a paper boy before becoming an entertainer.

Known for wearing a clock around his neck, William "Flavor Flav" Drayton was born in Roosevelt and is a classically trained pianist.

Melissa Joan Hart, who grew up in Sayville, was born without teeth on either side of her front teeth but had her teeth fixed in 1993. The daughter of a lobster wholesaler, Hart starred in her first commercial at age 4.

Eddie Money attended Trees High School in Levittown. Before entering the music industry, he was an NYPD patrolman. His brother is a retired NYPD sergeant.

Rosie O'Donnell of Commack, Long Island, says she watched television almost 24 hours a day after her mother died, when Rosie was only 10 years old. She was voted most popular at Commack High School South and worked in the catalog department of Sears.

CRAZY FOOD

Having played deejay at house parties
since age 16, graduated from the New
York Restaurant School, and learned
the ins and outs of the city's catering
business, Mark Weiss founded an
entertainment company at which he
deejays parties while simultaneously
preparing a gourmet meal. Now known
as DJ Chef, he's worked events for

clients such as Pepsi, Tommy Hilfiger, Gucci, Madison Square Garden, and Mercedes-Benz.

◆

Whoopi Goldberg stocks up on North Fork Potato Chips, kettle-cooked by third-generation Long Island potato farmers, at Murray's Cheese Shop in Manhattan.

◆

"Barefoot Contessa" Ina Garten was working in the White House Office of Management and Budget when on a whim she drove to the Hamptons to look at a specialty food store she saw listed for sale in the *New York Times*.

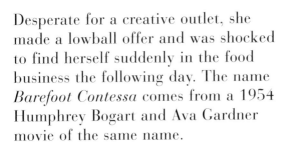

Desperate for a creative outlet, she made a lowball offer and was shocked to find herself suddenly in the food business the following day. The name *Barefoot Contessa* comes from a 1954 Humphrey Bogart and Ava Gardner movie of the same name.

In January 2009, restaurant business in Long Island was down 35 percent and Frank Minier, owner of Laguna Grille on Jericho Turnpike in Woodbury, was determined to come up with an economic stimulus package of his own. His solution? He offered a free meal worth $87.99 twice a day for four months. "It's our campaign to make sure that at least once in your lifetime you too can get a chance to get a 'bailout,'" the restaurant's Web site reads.

◆

When asked by a *New York Times* reporter in 2004 how she handled getting her famous North Fork Potato Chips out to stores and markets, Long Island potato farmer Carol Sidor laughed and said, "Distribution is me and my car!"

◆

There are more than 700 pizzerias on Long Island.

At the Best Pizza on Long Island Contest and Festival in 2005, "Skinny Mike" Hoffman ate an entire pizza in minutes. He won the Golden Pizza Slicer Award and $100.

◆

After opening Bobby's Burger Palace in Lake Grove in 2008, the Food Network star Bobby Flay joked about how his gig on *Iron Chef*, personalized line of condiments and cookware, and eight successful cookbooks couldn't satisfy his longing for a tasty little beef joint of his own. "Chefs have funny dreams," he told reporters. "They may have a couple of four-star restaurants, but they fantasize about opening up a little hot dog stand.... Now that I've gotten to this point, I can do the thing I crave the most—which is a cheeseburger, fries, and a shake."

◆

Richard Rubin of Baiting Hollow Farm Vineyard in Baiting Hollow, Long Island, is a former vice president of Weight Watchers.

◆

At Green Field Brazilian Steak House in Farmingdale, each table is equipped with a red light and green light. When diners want their servers to stop bringing new foods by for them to sample, they simply switch on the red light and enjoy what is already on their plates.

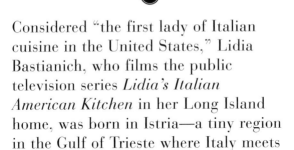

Considered "the first lady of Italian cuisine in the United States," Lidia Bastianich, who films the public television series *Lidia's Italian American Kitchen* in her Long Island home, was born in Istria—a tiny region in the Gulf of Trieste where Italy meets the former Yugoslavia.

◆

Riverhead's Martha Clara Vineyards hosted a *Guitar Hero* Tournament in February 2009, donating $100 to the winner's school music program.

Fox News' Greta Van Susteren is co-owner of the Old Mill Inn in Mattituck and occasionally stands in as a guest bartender.

◆

Cynthia Pereles sued a New York Applebee's restaurant in 2006 when the wait staff allegedly served her 5-year-old a Long Island Iced Tea instead of apple juice. She realized something had gone wrong when the child began laughing uncontrollably and wouldn't listen to her instructions to sit down and be quiet.

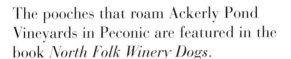

The pooches that roam Ackerly Pond Vineyards in Peconic are featured in the book *North Folk Winery Dogs*.

◆

Mattituck's Bouke Wines founder Lisa Donnenson met her husband while studying in Italy. One of the first things they did together was pick grapes in the Tuscan Hills.

CRAZY LIGHTHOUSES

The Huntington Harbor Lighthouse at the entrance to Lloyd Harbor and Huntington Harbor was destroyed by fire on November 12, 1947, when hunters spending the night inside let the fire they lit in the fireplace get out of control.

Originally located on a shoal when it was built in 1890, Cold Spring Harbor Lighthouse was deactivated and plans were made to tow it to Eaton's Neck and burn it. A local resident interested in town history bought it from the city for $1 and moved it to her private property in 1965.

◆

Margaret Buckridge Bock, daughter of Montauk Point Lighthouse keeper Thomas Buckridge, wrote an article for *The Beacon* in 1987 recalling how loud it was growing up with foghorns above her home. "Nobody has a conception of fog unless they have lived at the Montauk Lighthouse," she said. "Sometimes, the fog engines would run steadily for a week to 10 days. All the pictures on our walls would be crooked."

◆

Although the Cold Spring Harbor Lighthouse was rescued from destruction, its relocation had its own drama. The new owners put the lighthouse on a barge to move it to their property, but it became stuck on a sandbar. After all efforts to dislodge it failed, they had to wait almost a year for the water to rise to a sufficient level to float the barge and complete the trip.

Built in 1796, while George Washington was president, the Montauk Point Lighthouse was the first lighthouse ever established in New York state. Electricity and plumbing were not introduced there until 1938. The lens had to be wound by hand every 4 hours until an electric motor was installed in 1961.

◆

The current light at Montauk Point can be seen up to 19 nautical miles away. That's the power of 2.5 million candles.

In 1918, the ice at Cold Spring Harbor Lighthouse was so severe that it made the structure "sway, crack, and tremble tremendously," according to keeper Louis P. Brown. The beating of the ice against the lighthouse caused doors to open on their own and dishes to fall off the shelves.

◆

When Arthur Jensen was the keeper at Cold Spring Harbor Lighthouse during 1908, he had several visits from President Theodore Roosevelt, who would row his children into the harbor from his nearby summer home at Sagamore Hill.

Legend holds that Execution Rocks Lighthouse in Long Island Sound is named after Revolutionary War brutality, when British soldiers would tie their prisoners to the rocks and wait for the high tide to drown them. On February 4, 1920, the lighthouse became famous when a steamer wrecked, its stern nearly hitting the building, and the 14 horses on board spent three days waiting to be rescued. When drinking water ran out at the station, the keeper had to start melting snow for the animals to stay hydrated.

◆

Sands Point Lighthouse keeper Thomas J. Murray was scolded in June 1922 for having so many people come visit him

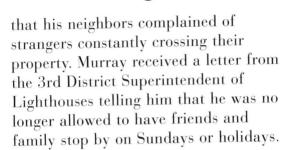

that his neighbors complained of strangers constantly crossing their property. Murray received a letter from the 3rd District Superintendent of Lighthouses telling him that he was no longer allowed to have friends and family stop by on Sundays or holidays.

◆

William Randolph Hearst bought the Sands Point Lighthouse for $400,000 in 1927 but later gave the title to the Dime Savings Bank to pay off his mortgage.

In 1869, many of the lantern panes at Shinnecock Bay Lighthouse on Ponquogue Point had to be replaced because birds kept running into them and cracking the glass. The entire building was later demolished.

◆

The Long Bar Beach Lighthouse off the western end of Orient Beach State Park is nicknamed Bug Light because its original 1870 steel frame makes the light look like an insect.

◆

Commissioned by Colonel George Washington in the 1750s, Horton Point Lighthouse in Southold was used to spy on incoming enemy aircraft during World War II.

◆

In April 1999, the Coast Guard couldn't find a 1-rpm motor to replace the one that had broken at Horton Point, so they instead installed a 2-rpm unit and blacked out every other lens, allowing the light to retain its characteristic flash every 10 seconds.

◆

The National Register of Historic Places incorrectly lists Stratford Shoal Lighthouse, also known as Middleground, as a Connecticut fixture. While it is located on a shoal between

Bridgeport, Connecticut, and Port Jefferson, New York, it is in fact a Long Island landmark.

◆

Eaton's Neck Lighthouse on the east end of Huntington Bay is the only Long Island tower still using a Fresnel lens.

◆

Stepping Stones Lighthouse keeper Charles A. Rogers was trapped in 17 inches of snow during one of Nassau County's infamous snowstorms in 1934. With only 2 days' worth of food on hand, he hung his flag upside down in hopes that someone would see the strange symbol and stop by to check on

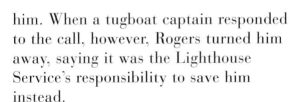

him. When a tugboat captain responded to the call, however, Rogers turned him away, saying it was the Lighthouse Service's responsibility to save him instead.

◆

American Indian folklore tells the tale of a Siwanoy tribe that fought with the devil, also known as Habboamoko, for the rights to Connecticut. Habboamoko was losing the battle until he looked over his shoulder and noticed a trail of stones, which he used to hop over to Long Island. As he made his way back across the water, he tossed every boulder at his enemies, giving all of New England new rock formations with his poor aim. Today the rocks and reefs along Long Island Sound, near Stepping Stones Lighthouse, are known as Devil's Belt or Devil's Stepping Stones.

◆

The light at the Sands Point Lighthouse originally displayed flashes of light, but it was changed to a fixed white light to distinguish it from the Execution Rocks Lighthouse light.

◆

Dean Kamen, inventor of the Segway Scooter, owns the North Dumpling Lighthouse in Fishers Island Sound.

Plum Island Lighthouse cannot be accessed by the public because it is surrounded by the United States Department of Homeland Security's Animal Disease Center.

◆

When it was built in 1827, Fire Island Lighthouse on the National Seashore was built right at the ocean's edge. Since then, the lapping waves have added 5 miles of beach between the lighthouse and the water.

◆

A spooky tale reports that more than 100 years ago, the caretaker at Fire Island Lighthouse hung himself and has haunted the place ever since. Even though the original building was knocked down and replaced with something taller in 1858, true believers claim to have seen the top windows of the lighthouse—which are inaccessible to visitors—open on their own.

◆

The Gardiners Island Lighthouse, built on a shaky sandbar 3 miles north of Gardiners Island near the former site of Fort Tyler, had to be abandoned in 1894 after a storm; its masonry fell into the sea within the year. Later, despite its reputation, the United States government spent $500,000 putting Fort Tyler on the same land to protect Long Island during the Spanish-

American War. But again, the sand was
unstable. New York State later bought
the property for a mere $50.

CRAZY PHENOMENA

Oyster Bay schoolteacher Tom D'Ercole claims that in the summer of 1975, a mysterious dark cloud hovered above his house and spit a stream of water at him as he headed for his car. He said the cloud changed shape, moved around, and enlarged to become around 6 feet tall. After soaking D'Ercole, the cloud disappeared.

A bizarre creature nicknamed by locals as the Montauk Monster washed up on a Long Island shoreline in July 2008 and again in May 2009. While an anonymous tip was sent to Gawker.com suggesting there was "a government animal testing facility very close by," no one could agree whether the creatures looked more like dogs, rodents, or small bulls, though many scientists seem to agree that both were raccoons.

◆

The old Sayville high school, formerly referred to as the Old 88, is rumored to have trapped dozens of children inside when it burned to the ground years ago. Today, rumor says, the children's souls haunt the school as ghosts and demons trying to drag people down into the afterlife.

◆

Teenagers in Sayville challenge each other to visit the grave of a girl named Lorelei at midnight. She was killed by her boyfriend and is rumored to haunt the area every evening.

◆

A ghostly opaque man uses a hoe to till the soil at an old farm along Broadway Avenue in Sayville.

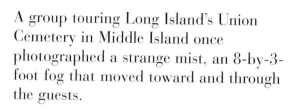

A group touring Long Island's Union Cemetery in Middle Island once photographed a strange mist, an 8-by-3-foot fog that moved toward and through the guests.

◆

There is a portrait at the Hewlett House in Old Bethpage Village that some claim will follow you with its eyes no matter where you go in the room. One visitor to the home said she felt an intense pull to walk around and found a noose hanging at the top of the stairs. Another claimed to feel a force trying to push her down the stairs. The pair held a séance and said they spoke with former homeowner Lewis Hewlett, who admitted to being the person who hanged himself overhead.

Also in Old Bethpage Village, the Williams House, which was once home to a seamstress named Esther, houses large trunks that have been found moved and opened, with their contents strewn about.

◆

The staff of trivia association Long Island Oddities once investigated claims that the Pizza Hut in Centereach was haunted by the ghost of a man who was killed in the men's room before the building became a pizza parlor. The manager claimed she could not keep pans from falling off the shelves and even tried tying them into place to prevent the cluttered mess.

After a schooner named the *Louis V. Pace* crashed in stormy winter weather off the Long Island Sound in February 1895, looters dragged the bodies of seven white men and one black man ashore. Assuming the African American was not a Christian, they buried him in the sand and took the others off for burial at the Lakeview cemetery in Patchogue. When they realized the African American was actually the ship's chef and a devout Christian, they returned to dig him up and repay their respects with another funeral. But they couldn't find the body. People soon began reporting seeing a black man walking the beaches in a peacoat whistling a ghostly tune. Whistling Sam, as he was called, seemed to disappear for good around 1953.

A Long Island folktale claims a group of boys were kidnapped and taken to Camp Hero, near the Montauk Lighthouse, to be brainwashed and taught how to use "the power of the mind" to perform telepathy and other amazing feats, such as jumping from buildings and airplanes without parachutes. During one session, the story goes, a fourth-dimensional monster was accidentally summoned by one of the children, and it killed everyone in the room.

◆

Legend holds that if you smell apples and cinnamon coming from the kitchen at Raynham Hall in Oyster Bay, the spirit of a servant woman welcomes you.

The room of a Revolutionary War officer's lover in Raynham Hall is always 4 to 5 degrees cooler than the rest of the house.

Years ago, the Swiss Embassy had a staff member staying at the Chandler Estate in Mount Sinai, and local church members gossiped that the Swiss flag flying outside was satanic. Nothing had been heard of the story until a resident returned home to find a group of mysterious children waiting for him, saying, "We're going to get you, devil man."

A man who worked at D.S. Shanahans
bar in Kings Park claimed to have seen a
woman disappear right in front of his
eyes in the hallway. The story is
enhanced by the fact that the bar sits on
the grounds of an old mental institution.

◆

Visitors have heard moaning and
footsteps at Fire Island Lighthouse in
Islip. The sounds are believed to be those
of a mourning keeper who had to wait 3
days for doctors to get to his family when
one of his daughters died from exposure
to cold weather.

Some people claim a woman in white roams the side of the road along Mount Misery and occasionally jumps out in front of cars.

◆

Drivers on Sweet Hollow Road in Melville honk their horns three times as they pass under the Northern State Parkway overpass. If they fail to honk, it is said that two ghost boys will jump out at them.

◆

Al Bielek claims to have experienced time travel as part of the alleged Montauk Project at Montauk Air Force Station, reportedly a U.S. government project to

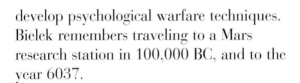

develop psychological warfare techniques. Bielek remembers traveling to a Mars research station in 100,000 BC, and to the year 6037.

CRAZY SPORTS

Hockey great Ray Ferraro's nicknames are Chicken Parm and The Big Ball of Hate. While with the National Hockey League, he scored 408 goals and had 490 assists, totaling 898 points in 1,258 games. He earned the name Chicken Parm after his retirement while working for the ESPN broadcast *NHL 2Night*, when he spilled his dinner moments before going on the air.

◆

Before joining the Long Island Rough Riders soccer team, legendary goalkeeper Tony Meola, who had already spent time playing professional soccer in England, announced he'd be taking some time off to star in the Broadway play *Tony and Tina's Wedding*. In 1999, he tried out to be a placekicker for the National Football League's New York Jets.

◆

Long Island's Jerome Travers became the second amateur to ever win the U.S. Open on June 18, 1915.

Venezuelan soccer star Giovanni Savarese moved to the United States to play at Long Island University and later signed on with the Rough Riders.

◆

When the New York Islanders hockey franchise was introduced in Nassau Couny, the team had to pay a $4 million territorial fee to the New York Rangers.

◆

Billy Harris was the first player ever drafted by the New York Islanders hockey team.

The first captain for the New York Islanders, Ed Westfall, also scored the team's first goal. Unfortunately, they lost the match to the Atlanta Flames 3-2.

◆

Montreal native Mike Bossy of the New York Islanders is the only hockey player other than Wayne Gretzky to score 50 or more goals for nine seasons. Unlike Gretzky, however, Bossy scored them in consecutive seasons.

◆

Jose Theodore is the only National Hockey League goalie to score a goal in an NHL game at Nassau Coliseum.

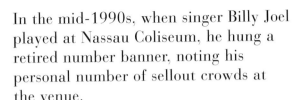

In the mid-1990s, when singer Billy Joel played at Nassau Coliseum, he hung a retired number banner, noting his personal number of sellout crowds at the venue.

◆

When it was built in 1923, the West Side Tennis Club was the first permanent tennis stadium in the United States.

◆

Employees of Babylon's Argyle Hotel formed the first African-American baseball team in history, the Cuban Giants, in 1885, to play against semiprofessional white teams.

The Long Island Ducks baseball team holds the independent league baseball single-season attendance record of 443,142 fans. The 3 millionth fan walked through the gates in September 2006.

◆

After upsetting fans with his controversial comments in the media in 2000 (which were considered racist, sexist, and homophobic), baseball's John Rocker (who played for the Atlanta Braves in 2000) tried to renew his career 5 years later by signing with the Long Island Ducks. But after 2 months, he withdrew his commitment, citing his pitching, which wasn't up to par.

The Ducks' Jose Offerman gained infamy on August 14, 2007, when he was hit by a pitch and responded by charging the mound with his bat and hitting Bridgeport Bluefish player Matt Beech in the hands. He then hit catcher John Nathans on the head before being taken into custody by police.

◆

America's first private golf course was founded when pro Willie Dunn developed a 12-hole course at Shinnecock Hills in Southampton in 1891.

◆

When the New York Islanders won four consecutive Stanley Cup Championships in the 1980s, fans nicknamed Nassau Coliseum "Fort Neverlose." Because of its deteriorating condition today, rival fans call it Nassau Mausoleum.

◆

Northport's Richie Hansen was the first native Long Islander to score a goal for the Islanders.

◆

The New York Islanders' uniforms at one time included a patch symbolic of the Montauk Lighthouse.

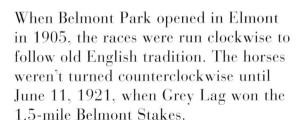

When Belmont Park opened in Elmont in 1905, the races were run clockwise to follow old English tradition. The horses weren't turned counterclockwise until June 11, 1921, when Grey Lag won the 1.5-mile Belmont Stakes.

◆

Only two hockey players, Pat Lafontaine and Jason Dawe, ever spent time on all three New York teams—the Islanders, the Rangers, and the Sabres.

◆

Julius Erving, also known as basketball's Dr. J, was born in Roosevelt and inducted into the Nassau County Hall of Fame in 2004.

Former Globetrotter Chris Sandy died in a car accident in Finland in November 2006 between seasons with the American Basketball Association's Strong Island Sound.

◆

Great Neck's Sarah Hughes beat out Michelle Kwan and Irina Slutskaya to win Olympic gold in ice skating at the 2002 games in Salt Lake City.

◆

Thoroughbred horse owner William McNight, best known as Tartan Stable, holds the record for the most number of wins at the Vosburgh Stakes held at Belmont Park in Elmont, with championships in 1967, 1968, 1969, and 1978. Angel Cordero Jr. holds the most number of wins by a jockey, with first-place finishes in 1973, 1978, 1983, 1984, 1987, and 1990.

◆

Uniondale was home to a professional women's soccer team under the Women's United Soccer Association, but the league suspended operations after just 2 years in 2003. Dubbed the New York Power, the original team included 1999 USA Women's World Cup players Tiffeny Milbrett and Christie Pearce.

Horse racing was first organized as an official sport when Richard Nicolls, the first English governor of New York, set up a course at Hempstead Plains. The first sweepstakes race was held 5 years later.

◆

In 2008, Melville attorney Ira Zaroff ran 120 miles nonstop from the Montauk Lighthouse to North Woodmere Park to raise money for Friends of Karen, a charity offering advocacy and financial help for the families of children being treated for life-threatening illnesses.

Originally named The Earth Day Marathon, The Long Island Marathon's first race was held in 1970.

◆

In 1750, more than 1,000 horses rode the Brooklyn ferry for the race at Newmarket Course at Hempstead Plains.

◆

One of the earliest sketches of 10-pin bowling is of a game being played in Suffolk County.

◆

In 1851, Long Island's George Steer built a ship for the New York Yacht Club to

race in England's Royal Regatta for the
first time.

◆

When a New York all-star team beat a
Brooklyn all-star team on July 20, 1858,
at Fashion Race Course on Long Island,
it was the first time admission (50 cents)
had ever been charged to attend a
baseball game.

◆

On June 30, 1899, Charles Murphy
gained the nickname Mile-A-Minute
when he rode his bicycle a mile on a
wooden track near Hempstead in 57.8
seconds.

The lowest winner's share in Belmont Stakes history was when The Finn earned $1,825 in 1915.

◆

There were five Belmont races in which only two horses entered the race: 1887, 1888, 1892, 1910, and 1920.

◆

Secretariat set the record for the fastest Belmont race when he ran a mile and a half in 2 minutes, 24 seconds in 1973.

◆

Hall of Fame outfielder Carl Yastrzemski, who hit 452 home runs and scored 3,419 base hits during his professional career, was born in Southampton.

◆

Houston Astros star Craig Biggio, who stole 414 bases during his 20-year career in the big leagues, was born in Smithtown and played both baseball and football at Kings Park High School in Suffolk County.

CRAZY CULTURE

Set in fictional Amity Island off the coast of Long Island, *Jaws* was directed by Steven Spielberg. Spielberg took friends Martin Scorsese, George Lucas, and John Milius to visit Bruce the Shark in the special effects shop of the movie, making the mouth clamp down on Lucas' head as a joke. The act, however, damaged the shark and caused technical difficulties during filming.

To keep from being dunked in the ocean by his crew on the last day of filming *Jaws*, Spielberg wore his most expensive outfit and jumped into a speedboat shouting "I shall not return" as soon as the final shot was captured.

◆

Denzel Washington turned down the role of Cinque in *Amistad*, the 1997 movie about a slave ship that ends up off the coast of Long Island. Cuba Gooding, Jr. also turned down the role, and Sean Connery said no to playing John Quincy Adams. Harry A. Blackmun, who played a United States Supreme Court justice, actually served as a real court justice from 1970 to 1994.

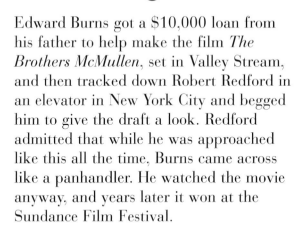

Edward Burns got a $10,000 loan from his father to help make the film *The Brothers McMullen*, set in Valley Stream, and then tracked down Robert Redford in an elevator in New York City and begged him to give the draft a look. Redford admitted that while he was approached like this all the time, Burns came across like a panhandler. He watched the movie anyway, and years later it won at the Sundance Film Festival.

◆

Filmed partially in Greenport, *The Devil's Own* starred Brad Pitt, who tried to leave the film after multiple rewrites, telling a *Newsweek* reporter the movie was a disaster and "the most irresponsible bit of filmmaking—if you can even call it that—that I've ever seen." He didn't have a choice, though, because the studio threatened him with a $63 million lawsuit if he walked.

◆

Actor Daniel Baldwin, who grew up in Massapequa, named his son Atticus after a character from his favorite movie, *To Kill a Mockingbird*.

◆

Massapequa native Alec Baldwin warned brother Stephen that taking a role in the 1996 Pauley Shore movie *Bio-Dome* could end his career.

After *Capturing the Friedmans* was filmed in Great Neck and Mineola, theater owners complained to distributor Magnolia Pictures that patrons refused to leave after the film was over, staying behind to argue the innocence of main characters Arnold and Jesse Friedman.

◆

The title of the movie *Eternal Sunshine of the Spotless Mind*, which was partially filmed in Montauk, is taken from the Alexander Pope poem "Eloisa" and was also used in *Being John Malkovich*.

◆

Roosevelt native Eddie Murphy asked the writers of *48 Hours* to change his character's name from Willie Biggs to Reggie Hammond because Biggs sounded too much like a "Hollywood made-up black guy's name."

◆

In the 2001 time travel period piece *Kate & Leopold,* Kate claims that she is "Kate McKay of the McKays of Massapequa."

◆

Long Beach native Billy Crystal's childhood dream was not to be a comedian but a professional baseball player. He was varsity captain of the Long Beach High varsity team his senior year and accepted a scholarship to play at Marshall University in West Virginia. He never played a single game, however, because the baseball program was suspended his freshman year.

◆

Billy Crystal's uncle, Milton Gabler, founded Commodore Records and produced Bill Haley's hit "Rock Around the Clock."

◆

Famous singer Billie Holiday babysat comedian Billy Crystal during his childhood days in Long Beach in the 1940s and 1950s.

For his 60th birthday, Long Island native Billy Crystal signed a 1-day contract with the New York Yankees and played against the Pittsburg Pirates as a designated hitter wearing the number 60. He hit one foul ball and then struck out.

◆

The lead role for the 1995 movie *Sabrina*, the story of a chauffeur's daughter who grew up on a fancy estate in Long Island, was originally offered to Winona Ryder, not Julia Ormond.

Actress Natalie Portman grew up in Syosset but was born in Jerusalem. She can speak Hebrew fluently and is partially conversational in French, German, Japanese, and Spanish. Portman once said she would never appear in a horror film or any other "Jennifer Love Hewitt type" of film.

CRAZY HAMPTONS

In 1725, Dick Syme was elected the Common Whipper of East Hampton and received 3 shillings for each person he whipped.

Sag Harbor used to be a bustling whaling port located partly in East Hampton and partly in Southampton. One town was dry and the other was wet, so the street dividing the two was named Division Street. Half of the bar at the end of the street served alcohol, and the other half did not.

◆

Some of Sagaponack's biggest names in real estate, media, and stockbrockering came together in 1998 to protest the building of one of the largest homes in the United States in their own backyards. Dubbing themselves the Sagaponack Homeowner's Association, they were concerned that a new multimillionaire in town had obtained a permit to build a 66,000-square-foot, 29-bedroom, 30-bathroom Italian villa as a single-family dwelling. Its garage could hold up to 100 cars. Its owner, Ira Rennert, was a quiet man, but his complex was on its way to becoming the largest in the Hamptons. His neighbors' greatest concern? Not that their oceanfront view would soon be compromised, but that Rennert, a dedicated Jew, would turn part of the building into an Orthodox synagogue.

◆

The oldest hotel in the Hamptons is the Baker House, formerly the J. Harper Poor Cottage. Built in 1648, it's one of the oldest continuously occupied structures in the United States.

A fan of Shakespeare, Baker House owner J. Harper Poor named the main house As You Like It after renovating it in 1911. When the remodel was complete, Poor rented a private train to bring guests in from Manhattan for his daughter's on-site wedding. The original invitation, gift book, and newspaper announcement still hang on the wall at Baker House.

◆

North Folk residents near the Hamptons' Baker House complained to the local legislative board in August 2008 that helicopters flying overhead were causing too much noise near their homes. "My 8-year-old has more restrictions riding her bike than these

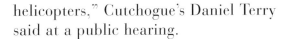

helicopters," Cutchogue's Daniel Terry
said at a public hearing.

◆

Long Island's Grey Gardens first
became famous when *New York
Magazine* uncovered the eccentric
residents living in total shambles there
in 1972. The property had deteriorated
so much that readers couldn't believe
the homeowners were Edith "Big Edie"
Ewing Bouvier Beale and Edith "Little
Edie" Bouvier Beale, who were the aunt
and cousin of Jacqueline Kennedy
Onassis. When it was raided by the
Suffolk County Health Department, the
home was hidden behind vines,
windows were broken, raccoon skulls
littered the floor, and more than 50

feral cats had been defecating around the premises.

◆

The father of the famous Baldwin brothers taught social studies and was a football coach in Massapequa. He also coined the town's nickname, Matzoh-Pizza.

◆

The oldest cattle ranch in the United States is Montauk's Deep Hollow Ranch.

◆

At the East Hampton town election on November 7, 1923, voters said no to appropriating $8,000 for bringing professional mosquito terminators into the town.

◆

East Hampton's Rod Anderson, Pam Brown, and Malcolm Brighton set off in a helium balloon from George Sid Miller's farm on September 20, 1970, attempting to become the first people to cross the Atlantic Ocean by hot-air balloon. Unfortunately, they crashed 500 miles from Newfoundland and everyone on board died.

◆

After he came to the Hamptons with the measles in 1798, Connecticut peddler

Ebenezer Dayton was tackled by four young men who shaved his head and dunked him in the town pond as punishment. Around 100 people in East Hampton contracted the measles, but to protest the way he was treated, Dayton sued the town for $1,000. His lawyer was future U.S. Vice President Aaron Burr.

◆

National Geographic voted East Hampton the Most Beautiful Village in the United States in 1968.

◆

In the mid-20th century, Sag Harbor was one of the busiest ports in the United States—almost as busy as New York itself.

Founded by farmers and fishermen from Connecticut, East Hampton was so religious that it held regular witchcraft trials in the 1600s. But no one was ever hanged or burned at the stake. Some of the town's English-inspired laws date back to King Charles I.

◆

Soak Hides Road got its name from a leather tannery once located there.

◆

Montauk, Amagansett, and Bridgehampton are not actually villages. They are hamlets, or unincorporated pieces of property.

Famous painter Jackson Pollock lived with his wife Lee Krasner in the East Hampton town of Springs. The Pollock-Krasner House and studio of the artist are now managed by the State University of New York at Stony Brook.

◆

The first three homes built in Montauk were named First House, Second House, and Third House. Used by men who tended cattle, sheep, and horses, First House burned to the ground in 1909, Second House is still standing in Montauk Village, and Third House is near Montauk State Park.

In 1931, the East Hampton Town Board voted 4-2 to spend $45 million for a floating bridge from North Haven to Shelter Island and from Shelter Island to East Marion in hopes that the new means of transportation would help locals find work during the Great Depression. To this day the town is still waiting for construction to begin.

◆

According to EastHampton.com, East Hampton's first juvenile delinquent was Daniel Fairfield, who was arrested in the mid-1600s for exposing himself in public (with two of his friends), for bursting into a schoolhouse and

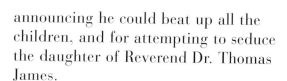

announcing he could beat up all the children, and for attempting to seduce the daughter of Reverend Dr. Thomas James.

Some of the first things printed in Long Island's first newspaper, the *Long Island Herald*, were sermons on lying and a remedy for dueling, both written by Lyman Beecher, East Hampton's fourth minister.

◆

Sag Harbor native Polly Sweet was the first woman from New York state to cross the Great Plains looking for gold via prairie wagon, and later became the first American woman "on scene" where gold was first discovered in central California in 1848.

Before the Revolutionary War, East Hampton was a part of Connecticut.

◆

Long Island's Amagansett was the only United States city invaded by the enemy during World War II. After being dropped from a submarine onto Atlantic Avenue Beach, four Nazi spies were caught on board the Long Island Rail Road.

◆

East Hampton was spelled as one word (Easthampton) until the *East Hampton Star* began publishing it differently when the paper was founded in 1885.

The Clinton Academy in East Hampton opened its doors on January 1, 1785. In 1815, its greatest year, the private school enrolled 156 students, including some from the West Indies.

◆

President Bill Clinton was refused golf privileges at Maidstone's Medway Golf Club in 2006 because ongoing midweek championships already crowded the course. One of the members was quoted as saying, "We can't deprive the paying members of their golf, even for an ex-president."

Suffolk County can fine restaurants between $50 and $500 for not clearly listing the price of specials on their menus. The bill passed in 2008 after area residents complained that too often they were embarrassed to ask the price of a specialty item in front of a date and then were surprised when they received their tab at the end of the meal.

◆

Agawam is the American Indian name for Southampton.

CRAZY CRIME

During a nasty divorce, Long Island surgeon Dr. Richard Batista demanded that his wife of 44 years return the kidney he donated to her or give him $1.5 million in compensation. He claimed that it was a last resort to regain control over negotiations in which he had been disallowed time with their three children. Unfortunately for

Batista, judges ruled that a kidney was now a permanent part of her body and not a "marital asset you can put a price tag on."

◆

In August 2007, more than $58,000 worth of parrots were stolen from Marc Morrone's Parrots of the World shop in Rockville Centre. Morrone said the theives brought their own cages but left them and took his. They also disabled security cameras and escaped through a hole in a window.

◆

When Dr. Charles Friedgood heard that his housekeeper had found his wife dead in her bed in June 1975, he rushed to his wife's side. But not to grieve. He was signing a death certificate claiming she had passed away of a stroke and was rushing to plan a funeral as soon as possible. After disappearing with $650,000 worth of her jewelry, he and his lover were caught by police in Denmark. It turns out that he had indeed planned his wife's death, injecting Demerol into her liver. Friedgood is still in prison serving his sentence of 25 years to life.

◆

Colin Ferguson was sentenced to 200 years in prison after gunning down passengers on a Long Island commuter train on December 7, 1993. A victim of extreme paranoia, he had long believed that white people were out to get him. Ferguson's lawyer proposed citing black rage as a defense, but Ferguson refused and maintained he was innocent. He later admitted to waiting until the train entered Nassau County before opening fire to keep from embarrassing New York City mayor David Dinkins.

◆

Brothers Wayne and John Dougal faced complaints from the town of Oyster Bay in early 2009 when the "stinky mountain of wood chips" sitting on their 18-acre property had area residents pinching their noses.

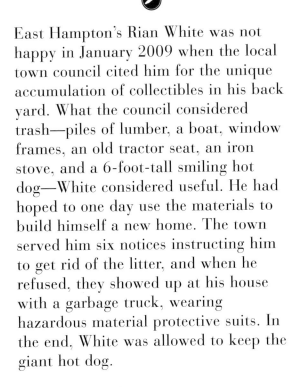

East Hampton's Rian White was not happy in January 2009 when the local town council cited him for the unique accumulation of collectibles in his back yard. What the council considered trash—piles of lumber, a boat, window frames, an old tractor seat, an iron stove, and a 6-foot-tall smiling hot dog—White considered useful. He had hoped to one day use the materials to build himself a new home. The town served him six notices instructing him to get rid of the litter, and when he refused, they showed up at his house with a garbage truck, wearing hazardous material protective suits. In the end, White was allowed to keep the giant hot dog.

In 1994, the federal government had to step in to help regulate the price of garbage and trash hauling on Long Island because the local mob had a hold on the market. Other companies that had come into town to try to compete found their customers intimidated and their trucks burned.

◆

Convinced that having a candy cigarette would increase the likelihood that a child would later switch to the real thing, Democrats in Nassau passed a bill in January 2009 ordering that candy and bubble gum versions of cigarettes be put behind the counters at retail outlets.

A Southold man called police in January 2009 asking to be arrested and deported back to his home country of Guatemala. When told he couldn't be arrested because he had not committed a crime, the 27-year-old kicked the officers' patrol car. It was deemed fourth-degree criminal mischief, and he was taken into custody.

◆

Long Island waiter Stephen Buttafuoco had no idea that the Arabic chants recorded on his cell phone would cause mass chaos at work. But when he pulled out his phone to show it off to a friend in January 2009, it ended up broadcasting over the loudspeaker at the Jewish wedding reception where he was serving hors d'oeuvres. The hundreds of guests thought the voices, which were actually from a pro-Palestinian rally in Manhattan, meant that they were under a terrorist attack. Buttafuoco was charged with commission of a hate crime, to which he pled innocent. He was, however, fired from his job.

◆

A Nassau County man was arrested in the fall of 2008 for renting out an empty home that was on the market to be sold. His leasers thought they were getting a great deal with the $1,000 per month rent until the actual owners showed up 2 weeks into the deal.

A West Babylon man secretly selling an illegal weapon shot his .22-caliber rifle out the window of his Massapequa home in early 2009 to prove to his potential buyer that it was in working order. While the bullet did not hit anyone, the shooter was charged with criminal possession of a weapon and reckless endangerment.

◆

In 2005, Nassau and Suffolk counties had half the crime that most United States counties had, with only 2,042 crimes per 100,000 residents.

◆

Thanks to complaints by local firemen who claimed Silly String had damaged the paint on their trucks and hydrants, the town of Huntington passed a measure in 2008 to ban the sale of the party product within 1,500 of any public festivity, especially parades.

◆

Long Island's Favorite Magician Robert Infantino, who once won $10,000 on ABC's *America's Funniest People*, was arrested in 2008 after secretly videotaping women undressing before getting their portraits taken at his home-based photography business in central Islip.

◆

During the late 1980s, when computers were gaining popularity in workplaces,

Suffolk County became the first U.S. county to implement a computer-usage law. The law required companies that used more than 20 VDTs, or video display terminals, to supply employees with 15-minute breaks every three hours, vision care, on-the-job safety training, and health education courses. A year after it was enacted, the New York State Supreme Court repealed the law.

◆

In 2002, the Southampton town board passed a law against hanging clothes on clotheslines in yards. Punishments for violating the law included a fine of up to $1,000 and a jail sentence of up to 6 months. The law was repealed.